Entanglements

Poems
Tony Magistrale

Paintings
Michael Strauss

Fomite
Burlington, Vermont

Poems copyright © 2013 Tony Magistrale
Paintings copyright © 2013 Michael Strauss

All rights reserved. No part of this book may be repro- duced in any form or by any means without the prior written consent of the publisher, except in the case of brief quotations used in reviews and certain other noncommercial uses permitted by copyright law.

This is a work of fiction. Names, characters, places and incidents are either the product of the author's imagination or are used fictitiously. Any resemblance to actual persons, living or dead, events or locales is entirely coincidental.

Every effort has been made, where necessary, to contact the copyright holders for permission to reprint borrowed material that is not in the public domain. We regret any oversights that may have occurred and would be happy to rectify them in future printings of this work. The publisher and the author make no representations or warranty, expressed or implied, including, without limitations, any implied warranty of merchantability or fitness for any purpose.

ISBN- 978-1-937677-43-5
Library of Congress Control Number: 2013933882

Fomite
58 Peru Street
Burlington, VT 05401
www.fomitepress.com
Cover painting - Michael Strauss

Entanglements

Contents

Part One: Letters to America 1

My Visit to the Alliance Church of Christian Rock .3
Night on Bread Loaf Mountain................................4
Moving Daze 5
A Good Time..7
The Rebel in Me 8
San Diego 10
What If the Whole World Were Las Vegas? 11
My Hometown...12
Crime Scene 13
Monster Man 14
We All Stand for Justice 15
Prisoner Exchange..17
View From My Hotel, Boston, December 1, 2011 ..19
Casualty..21
Everything Else 23
Blame 24
Letter to America 25

Part Two: Tangled Up in Blue 27

If...29
Girls in Cars..30
Saks Fifth Avenue, Ground Floor..........................31
Hat Check 33
Trouble at the Buddha's Altar 34
Knocking on Your Door..35

The Drive-In 37
The Massage 38
The Persistence of Memory 39
Since You Been Gone 40
Rituals of Elimination 41
Dear Jennifer Aniston 43
Tavern Portrait 44
Tonya Harding Agonistes 45
My McCarthy Era 47
Shadowland 48

Part Three: Innocent Abroad 49

Failure 51
Candyland 53
Why Language Matters 55
Schattenboxen 56
From the Tongues of Strangers 58
On Viewing Brueghel's *Hunters in the Snow* 59
Collusion 60
Reading Edgar 61
My Grandmother's Place 62
Frank Barone 65
Pool Table 66
Head Down 67
Then, the Letting Go 68

Part Four: Some Seasonal Excesses 69

Canada Snow Geese 71
Early Season Frost 72
Hurricane 73

The Winterscapes of Stockholm's Prins Eugens
Waldermarsudde Galleriet 74
Final Preparations 75
Harbingers 77
First Day of Winter 79
Day Spent Defining Superlatives 80
Warm Summer Wind 82
Lesson Learned 83
Vampire Redux 85
Watching Pornography 87
My Father's Cars 88
What's Coming 91
Entanglements 92
Acknowledgements 95

Two subatomic particles, once they have been in contact, will remain subtly entangled no matter how far they are separated in space.

John Stuart Bell's *Theorem of Quantum Mechanics*

The one thing no species can ever be is self-reliant. Being entangled is the condition of life itself.

Verlyn Klinkenborg

Part One: Letters to America

My Visit to the Alliance Church of Christian Rock

My wife cajoled me into attending last Sunday
with the promise of blueberry pancakes and crispy bacon
afterwards. We entered from the back
into a wave of amplified sound—guitars, synthesizer
and heavy drums—some middle-aged blonde
leading the congregation in delirious rhythms.
Although sexy enough in her tight black leather pants,
I couldn't help but think
this rocker chick fantasy had gone horribly askew.
For this was no Joan Jett homage,
no stoned head banger preaching the profane gospel
of sex and sordid temptation. Jesus had enfolded
His name seamlessly into every lyric, purifying each verse
like it had passed through a celestial censor,
providing all the white women up front divine uplift
as they grooved to the band's electrified ethereal riffs,
right hands raised in unanimous testimony towards heaven.
I recognized the Pentecostal salute
Aunt Becky's mother used to summon
whenever she beseeched the Lord to smite her many enemies.
In the end, they couldn't convert me with their
Christ is one Cool Dude karaoke;
I'm too old to buy into God going this soft.
And I can still spot a well-rehearsed rapture when I see it,
those dreamy eyeballs-rolled-back-into-the-head faces
swaying to the music next to me
may be high on sugar instead of wine,
but they're still hawking the way to salvation
the nuns tried to impart years ago
with their raised rulers
and a *Baltimore Catechism*'s cant.

Night on Bread Loaf Mountain

So many stars on view tonight from Bread Loaf mountain.
They make me wonder if it is as quiet
         up there

as it is down here
beneath those thousand ganglia clusters of light.
I know we should all be troubled
         by this implication—

after all, if God resides in a quieter place
than the dark line of woods that rim
         the horizon

or the invisible creek barely audible
meandering off into the open meadow,
         what might that imply?

The best of the beautiful in this world,
the kind that is impossible to ignore,
is always served up in
         distant silence:

think back to that woman
who never became your wife,
who never even suspected how often
         you thought about her.

Moving Daze

I catch myself at the edge of a foreboding
        a sudden nervousness,

like the unease others might feel
when they encounter a cop,
every time I see a moving van
idling in my neighborhood, or grinding its way lethargically
down the street. Residue anxiety
        would be my guess

from my own history of unsettling self-rupturings
in a country where no one
        stays in one place very long.

Cavernous metal boxes on wheels,
their massive doors swung open
to reveal the guts of lives being displaced
then reassembled elsewhere
        strange miles away,

like some cosmic jig-saw puzzle,

belie a future moving day
when furniture and kitchen utensils
will not be waiting curbside
and there won't be any new neighbors
        to meet.

A Good Time

The kid, not more than three or four,
is having himself a good time
turning around in his seat, chatting it up
with the other passengers, charming the crowded bus silly
so that some of us are talking back to the kid.
His mother, however, is not having such
a good time, as she leans into her girlfriend
and asks, *what kind of man walks out
on his family for another woman?* The kid
stares out the window and points,
*what are those pink things growing,
and why are puddles full of black rain?*
His mother either doesn't hear the questions,
or is dispossessed of any answers.

The Rebel in Me

There is a large window
in front of the desk where I write.
This window looks down on a busy street
where I enter into the lives of strangers
for thirty seconds or so
before they turn a corner, or disappear
into a car parked on either side of the street.

Every person I see is in transit—
home from the grocery store, on the way to school,
back to work. And everyone moves
with an exacting deliberation.

Except for this boy I watched yesterday
who was barely managing,
he looked like a miniature old man
instead of ten, stooped over by the weight
of his world. I mean this literally:

he carried schoolbooks that ballooned a backpack,
a bulbous musical instrument in one hand,
and in the other, a thick plastic tube
that might have contained inside
a map of the universe.

He bore a look of utter misery
down there alone, struggling against his Herculean burden,
sweating in simmering heat on the first day of summer.

The rebel in me was tempted to yell down
dump that backpack, take off your sweaty shirt,
sit down on the curb,
and play a few bars of something jazzy
up to me. But that might have
changed the whole tenor of this street,

disrupting its beehive of purposeful activity,
and left a scar on the kid
so deep he might have gone home
and told his parents to shove it;
tonight, he would do no homework.

San Diego

You have to wonder why such a beautiful place
keeps its garage doors closed
and its windows blind to the sun,

why the sudden appearance of a woman
standing alone in her driveway
dressed only in a white bathrobe
invokes, at least at first glance,
the suggestion of insurrection—or madness.

The identical crème-colored houses,
each with carefully manicured lawn and cactuses
maintained by olive-skinned hands,

hydrated islands in a river of smooth-winding streets
with names such as *Seafarer* and *Sunquest*.
In the absence of kids on bicycles,

rustless, expensive foreign automobiles
ferry neighbors to work, children to school,
and delicate blond wives
to shopping plazas and malls

while lonely white sidewalks await
the release of anxious small dogs.

What If the Whole World Were Las Vegas?

For Marci & Bert

The desert sun suspended in crystalline azure
would greet each uniform day

and time never again to be
regulated by clocks, so mundane.

The greatest places known to man
consigned to palaces of marble and gold,

why bother with a passport
when the entire world is already here to behold?

This city has a cure for loneliness
just a 1-800-GOODLVN call away

while out on Las Vegas Blvd.
everyone is Elvis, at least for a day,

and the whole family eats for $19.95
at the Endless Chicken Bucket Buffet.

Here at last fulfilled is the western promise
of plenitude, a cornucopia of hope,

where every sucker has a chance
and Thoreau was just a dope.

My Hometown

Transit Road was once a sea of corn
and open sky, an itinerary I remember
where birds actually stopped on their annual migrations.
This was before the sprawl,
oozing out of fast food restaurants
and gas stations with eighteen nozzles,
changed the configuration of acres into miles.
Somebody got very rich
transforming Transit Road, reallocating
trees and meadows to accommodate Progress,
this American vision where red suns
continue to set in spectacular displays,
but off in the distance, in the corner
of purple skies, as if embarrassed
or banished, I can't decide which.
The nineteen-year-old girl
majoring in Hospitality Management
also grew up here and can remember only
four lanes of highway and chicken delights,
unbroken tracts of white concrete and pastel shopping malls
stretching out so vast to the horizon
that it is impossible to walk anywhere
without being accosted by machines,
their time come around at last,
overconfident in the knowledge
that this is their town now
and you, an awkward intruder on asphalt turf.

Crime Scene

The cop shows have taken my television hostage
a nightly line up of criminologists, forensics, & SWAT teams
righting an array of dark atrocities,

subconsciously reaffirming to inert & terrified TV Land America
our collective vulnerability & need of police intervention.

Cops on TV don't bludgeon unarmed citizens because
they can. They are regular guys & gals
balancing superhero powers in uncomplicated harmony:

equally at home in soup kitchens & ballistics,
prone to violence yet psychologically nuanced,
holding compatible degrees in martial arts and marital therapy.

No TV cop is ever a drunk, on the take, or criminally insane.

Police dramas whet the insatiable American appetite
for a sip of ferocity before bed
tinged with a short moral chaser;
each creepy, sociopathic nut job
gets his fifty minutes of mayhem
as prelude to teary lock up, or bullet-riddled resolution.

If TV cops patrolled the world,
prostitutes would regenerate their virginity,
abandoned kids would get furnished apartments at Disneyland,
& Jesus would pack a .357 Magnum, just in case.

Meanwhile, the rest of us would behave

as if we lived in church
& spoke only with library voices.

Monster Man

Lead story on the 6 o'clock news last night
featured this guy who borrowed a black monster truck
with oversized tractor tires,
rode it down in broad daylight
to his local police station parking lot
and proceeded to rumble over the cherry tops of six
white cruisers purchased only last week
that had just been meticulously aligned
with red-stenciled letters P-O-L-I-C-E.
He flattened the roof of every car
on one run, then turned around
and ran over them all again
until each of two dozen tires popped flat,
like inflated paper bags
slapped shut by a savage hand.
When he was finished, the monster truck
drove him another mile down the road
to a convenience store market
where he purchased a monster cherry Slurpee
as part of some private celebration ritual,
and then got arrested by a cop
driving the only serviceable cruiser left in the fleet.
The coifed blond newscaster finished her report
with a head-shot of the alleged monster man;
he resembled a slightly fried version
of the Man of Sorrows, long greasy hair and beard,
a look of utter wonderment,
or horror behind those eyes,
impossible to ascertain which for certain.
My wife said, *that's one young man
with serious anger management problems,*
but all I could do was whisper back,
my hero.

We All Stand for Justice

In their unequivocal world of right and wrong,
we all stand for justice
pursued by overly determined men
wearing expensive suits with silk ties, and
women who strut like men in their black power
pumps and wear no makeup and seldom smile.
We all stand for justice
in this solemn and serious room
devoid of even a whiff of humor or irony,
where docket numbers are processed into the System
for various affronts the State has taken
personally: two hundred dollars
for smoking pot, a week for mouthing off
to a cop, probation for punching
your girlfriend in the face.
The suits prosecute boys and men
who are still boys, leaving each one
to hang his shaggy, stupid head in remorse.
We all stand for justice
and their collective failure to learn anything
since the last time they stood here
amidst promises never again
to have their miserable lives derailed
by some officious bureaucrat
whose identity is wrapped up inside a robe or uniform,
and who sincerely couldn't care less.

Prisoner Exchange

She calls on a Saturday morning,
hot July day full of ripening possibilities,
of pleasant summer distractions

I'm anticipating soon to indulge,
to inform me she's in jail
bereft inside the drunk tank,

arrested last night a mile outside of town
on her way to another meeting
when she stopped to pee

in woods by the edge of the road.
I'm now to bail her out—
first, to the bank, to get cash

because no check will solicit her discharge;
the cop guard instructs me,
go around to the back of the building, buddy,

*we'll let her out from behind the white
metal door.* And she does eventually emerge
looking sad and washed out, her disheveled hair

hanging dank and exhausted around her face,
no makeup, they've taken her purse;
she confesses, *I got nuthin' left*.

I stand silently alongside my little car—
she won't look me in the eye
more shamed by her relapse,

or our reunion in the shadow of this penitentiary?
She's close to letting go
all the tears she's managed so far to restrain

when I produce the white document
they have provided me in our prisoner exchange,
pull her into a long hard hug and tell her,

this paper says you still belong to me.

View From My Hotel, Boston, December 1, 2011

From out the window of my tall hotel
I peer into the guts of an office building,
revealing a bee hive cross-sectioned,
or a scene reminiscent of *Rear Window*,
where dozens of workers reside on a dozen floors
wearing white shirts and black ties,
white blouses and black skirts,
each seated in separate cubicles
staring at blue computer screens
that contain the black font of messages
and orders, or whatever it is
these workers are paid to process
for hours every day.

Every so often, one of the workers
will exit his or her chair, rising up
to walk across the expanse
of brightly-lit floor
to another cubicle.

Just to talk.

I do not think
any of the many windows
in the office building
across from my hotel
can be made to open.

Casualty

The pert blond evening news lady
sporting new hair extensions
insists he was one of us,
played ball in high school, loved his mother
and girlfriend, too. Jump cut to clean-shaven head
shot followed by his number
in the assembly of numbers,
ambushed or blown to unrecognizable bits,
sacrificed for us who love to bully war
and have grown accustomed to the fact
that our flags fly at half-mast half the time.
The newscasters never offer
details about why he died,
or whose interests he fought to protect,
just another casualty of war
on its last, somber journey to a plot in Arlington.
Some kid from Arizona or Vermont,
son of a car salesman, a farmer's daughter,
but never the child of a politician
or corporate juggernaut. Just
another scared soldier in a strange place
trying to keep his head down
and not be a hero, who couldn't
speak the language or assimilate
the culture, but got swept up
by choices that were never his own.
After the actual dying, the worst casualty
is in the truism every warrior who has ever fought
hears from those who always remain behind:
we appreciate
your sacrifice
for the country's honor and good,
and there was never any other way.

Everything Else

There are plenty of dollars
for everything they requisition—computerized
war craft that simulates angry birds of prey,
Homeric armies that search and destroy,
more prisons. Excluded

from the privileged circle
everything else has gone to shit—
bridges reveal their skeletal underframes
rust burnt orange,
the roads upon which we drive
explode in an acne of
pot holes.

Our truest concession to globalization
is a third-world mass transit system,
and for fifty million
the real terror threat
is getting sick. Some

where within the designated web,
safe from the Islamic
jihad, they forgot to protect
everything else.

Blame

Black and silver televised plumes
beamed up from underwater robotics—
could be space as easily as gulf-bed floor—
underscore the helplessness of our fate,

technological wizardry that goes only so far.
Trapped in sci-fi nightmare, each day
earth's ruptured hole bleeds unimpeded
staining the sea above the color of blood

—for good reason. One day's waste:
5000 barrels of pressurized crude
5000 feet down = 5 minutes
of total oil consumption in Texas.

And we look in vain
for someone to blame.

Urged on by the most voracious among us
corporations drill day and night
turning oceans and beaches into
dead zones, suffocating aquatic habitats

that took eons to formulate
with the dark ooze of petrochemicals
squeezed up from the earth's teat
until the death circle completes itself—
organic life dies and decomposes

then, like some avenging ghost,
finds compressed release, and rises up
again to kill. And we look in vain
for someone to blame.

Letter to America

America, can we get a few things
straight between us and both agree
to stop taking you so seriously? Can we
at least recognize that many immoral people
are responsible for all the current level of sanctimoniousness
affiliated with you? Do we really want them representing your
image around the globe? After all,
how many of them were ever capable
of appreciating your ironic side—like first filling the world
with guns and violence and prisons,
and then staking a claim to
religious exceptionalism? America,
you can't be a God-fearing officious cop to the universe
and a stand-up comedian, all at the same time.
You simply must choose.
America, this is no time for moral platitudes—
not when there's big money to be made.
Let's come back to some salient points
upon on which we can agree.
America, strip off your sweaty grownup
clothes, your adult suits and ties,
your high heels and makeup, and for once
exhale. Tonight, watch the pretty bruised purple sunset
through the mist of fluorocarbons
without trying to figure out how
to make money off of it.
America, yesterday one of your troubled sons
tried to run away from his job
as a flight attendant on an airplane
filled with cranky, overheated people.
He flew out the door atop a rubber
chute, beer in hand, and instead of applauding his rebel yell,
you arrested him and charged him with
Reckless Endangerment.
Let's try to be honest here, America.

What part of his decision was
reckless? And what exactly did he
endanger? If we can't get you to recognize
a sincere quest for freedom
as one of your founding principles,
we should all be back wearing chains.
His leap made the national news
and, once again, we were all left wondering:
should we laugh or cry? America, one out of every
hundred of your huddled masses now resides in prison,
one out fifity-five is enmeshed in your penal colony.
We should definitely work on your priorities:
fix your own crumbling infrastructure
instead of every country in the Middle East,
find your citizens some jobs that do not entail
working for the penal system or toxic waste disposal,
and above all else, try to cultivate a sense of humor
until it crosses over into the absurd, or
neither one of us
is likely to survive any of this much longer.

Part Two: Tangled Up in Blue

If

You were to walk with me into the country
along an empty tree-lined road
with deep piles of snow on either side
the black fingers of elongated limbs
poised like cracks
against a seamless purple ceiling
and if somewhere
in the middle of this road
I were suddenly
to pull you close to me
your surprise registered in our
silver breaths blending
as I slipped inside
your winter overcoat
lifting you up to my mouth
until the tips of your
thin boot heels
left the earth completely
your lips
chilled by night air
would instantly warm.

Girls in Cars

Dusk. The blue hour is upon us.
And with it, a stillness that concludes
this late August afternoon
as we drive slowly, top down, the radio playing softly,
something soulful from Springsteen.

You are next to me in a little summer dress,
all sun-kissed brown, two shades of honey-blond lighter,
big sunglasses, shiny lips
you have painted when I wasn't looking,
happy as a big red bow. I confess
I have wished to fast-forward to this moment
for what seems my entire life,
inspired by girls riding in the front seats of cars
driving the long lengths of empty boulevards at night
their hair swept back in summer wind,
faces half-shadowed beneath halogen street lights,
always sitting close to some other boy.

But not tonight. Tonight,
that poignant trunkful of adolescent longing
is as far away as the stars blinking on above us.

How right it feels to lean in close
and steal another kiss,
to seal this perfect day spent together
and store it, like a farmer's sweet-smelling hay
stashed for some winter day
when white winds will be arctic fierce
and the seat next to mine
once again empty.

Saks Fifth Avenue, Ground Floor

He is the only male circling awkwardly
the perimeters of the cosmetics department.
Into this estrogen canyon he meanders
past slinky women heavily adorned under their own products,
like it was opening night at the opera
instead of 11 a.m. on Wednesday,
and up to the Chanel counter.
The woman working there blinks mauve-lidded
eyes at him, signaling a combination curiosity
and bemusement, as if he is some lost child
strayed from a distracted mother's hand.
In *sotto voce* he surrenders himself to her
expert counsel: *the exact lipstick, please,*
she *used to wear,*
a faint hope that possession of this Chanel talisman
might compel her back home.
A chasm of silence opens between them.
The saleswoman bites her lower magenta lip
in sympathy, but also recognizes
a ship-wrecked sailor even absent his island,
tells him, *Honey, wouldn't you be better off*
buying a jar of our vanishing cream?

Hat Check

At the bottom of a February
snow-packed and cold,
she sends me photographs
of herself self-adorned,
one wearing this big floppy hat
festooned with long black ostrich feathers,
face barely visible
behind oversized sunglasses.
The only way I am certain it is her
is the shape of her mouth—
I'd know those lips anywhere,
even disguised under a fiery magenta,
could pick them out of any
lipstick line-up. I can't decode
where she's going in that outfit—
if she's engaged in girlish play
at being a movie star, homage
to some Hollywood femme fatale,
holding lit cigarette in the fingers of long
black gloves; perhaps this is her Lenten costume,
an early start on *Carnivale*. She may be
running away from an errant lover, on the lam
from some palooka she quit on.
The photograph proves unyielding, her mystery cloistered,
another reminder, as if I needed one,
of all the women she contains
under her hat.

Trouble at the Buddha's Altar

I endeavor to follow the Path
of the Buddha. Centering Being on regulated

heart beats, practicing Patience and Resignation
to Powers greater than myself. Then,

You send out Word
of a future Meeting between Us

sure to involve so much more than copasetic
minds and spirits, promising an Array of secular

Diversions—beginning with the sharp Taste of your perfume
inside my Mouth—certain to distract me so Far

from the quiet repose of a body at Perfect Rest
that the Buddha throws up his ancient arms in weary

Frustration, while I Surrender
to a whole different set of Breathing Priorities.

Knocking on Your Door

Our time together has come to resemble
less the raging cataract it was
than a strong, steady stream in spring,
a place where I am comfortable
swimming naked, although always
alert to potential undertow.

Those Saturday afternoons
when I would forgo my usual exercise routine
in favor of exercising with you.
The mere proximity to your door
enough to set my heart adrift in white water;
the excruciating wait for you to come answer
as though each of my arrivals a surprise—
your hair an uncombed sweep of blond,
one eye lined with mascara, the other not;
one shoe on, the other buried in cluttered closet.
Only a lover would remember
such indelicate details—not to skewer
your half-hearted apologies,
but to confess savoring a wondrous
incompleteness: pupa caught in transit
from chrysalis to glory,
catching you half-dressed
on your way to undressed.

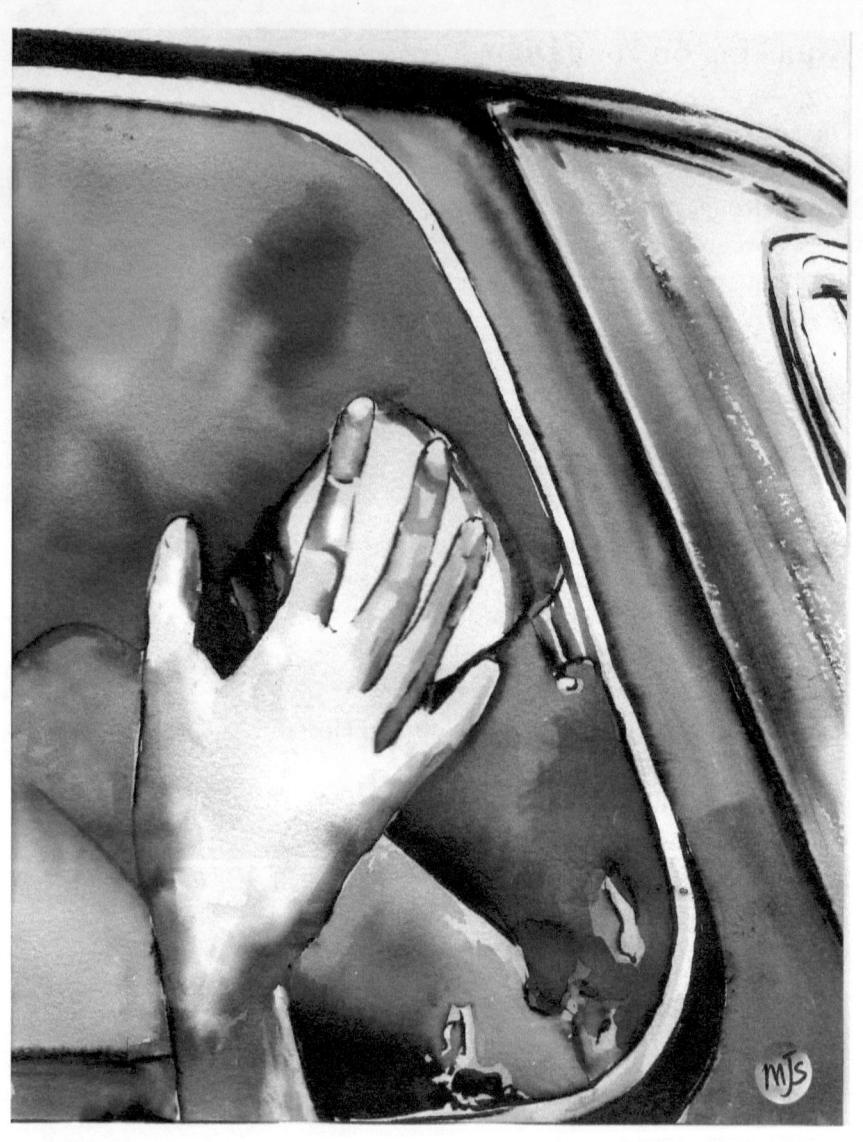

The Drive-In

Colleen Dolan and I spent Friday nights in high school
not watching movies from the back seat
of my father's green Oldsmobile—purple crushed velour,
like the upholstered furniture
in my mother's parlor. I never once dared
to touch those chairs or sofa
with my naked buttocks
even though they were securely condomed in plastic,
removable only on holidays and for important
adult guests.

The movies we paid to see—
The Graduate, Getting Straight, Beach Blanket Bingo—
a simulacrum to the action
going on inside the car,
our teenage experiments with vodka
and orange juice, the unscripted fumblings
in a makeshift bedroom,
last row back where the cinders ended
and the pine trees sucked in breath sharply
each time the wind blew.

We were anchored to the earth
only by a silver metal speaker,
its static sputtering of sound and dialogue
hovering, alongside the face of the moon,
our late night voyeur, pressed tightly
against the car's cool window
watching the two of us
stutter across thresholds in the dark.

The Massage

Tucked inside its own envelope,
candle-lit room floats above
November-darkened street. Inside,
warmed oils and scented creams
massage this body that should hold
no new mysteries. Yet, tonight,
it feels new to me—not strange or uncomfortable,
even in this dim light—but
different, as though the individual
parts belonged to some other
woman, not a lover.

I am committed to places
where lovers seldom linger:
stretching hamstrings and kneading
shoulder muscles, applying steady pressure
to the soles of size 8 feet,
so smoothly elegant when I view them
inside your tall boots and shiny stilettos,
but naked, surprisingly calloused,
complex. Time unfolds—
your body unwinds and opens. You have
more secrets yet to reveal as you gradually unlock
under the caress of my greasy, laboring fingers,
a yellow flower in the dusk, slowly
shedding workday toils, like pedals
dropping off against summer rain.

The Persistence of Memory

What better reminder of the danger
than Lot's wife, looking back over lovely
shoulder, punished for a last glance back.
So, how to explain
our own compulsion to recollect
scent of a receding perfume—
at once precious and precarious,
that seduces at the same time as it exhausts?

An unexpected break-up—
its drama continuing to unfold darkly
entering euphoric Christmas party ambiance—
her drunken, slurred, stumbling, sprawling;
skirt ratcheted to mid-thigh, stocking split
in long sutured gash, smudged mascara
under eyes red-blotched and desperate.

*Why are you doing this? Is this
what you want? Why won't you talk to me?*
It could have been either of us
asking, but this final time it was her
as she skated on wet snowmelt across wooden floor,
boot heels suddenly too high, too thin,
propelling her into startled revelers.
Amid the pendulous thrashing of
lanky arms and legs once adored,
reduced now to a prurient interest
from strangers eagerly assembling
to watch whatever was left disassemble.

What persists in memory
was my urge to disappear
from this terrible junction—
pity at the intersection of shame.

Since You Been Gone

I didn't do it deliberately,
set out to drive by your old house to note its black
windows staring vacantly back at me, the little brown flower garden
you tended the last year you lived there. I didn't expect
to spend time looking at any of this on such a golden
Saturday in October, the sky bluer than your eyes,
but there I stood
my hands in my pockets motionless
across the street from the big maple tree in the front yard
its leaves bleeding red up against that empty blue sky,
a combination so bright it almost hurt to look.
But I did: drank it all down
like a glass of cold cranberry juice, bitter
as it was sweet,
and stayed there long enough
to watch as a small breeze flipped each leaf
halfway across itself like little discs of fire,
enough beauty to distract me
from the rest of your abandoned yard:
the dead leaves scattered on the ground below,
those few left clinging to black sticks high above,
reminding me of old men standing alone
at a bar or in the middle of an empty road
confused, refusing to go home even though they know
they have had too much to drink
because they have lost their way somehow,
have forgotten what home is supposed to feel like now,
or just knew too many women who upped
and moved away.

Rituals of Elimination

He makes a list of things he should have
done months ago. First, the deletion of all her
photographs and emails from his computer's storage,
as if her lingering presence there
constitutes a virus that threatens the machine's life.

Next, the erasure of her phone
numbers, home and cell, from his book
containing the numbers of family
and friends, the supermarket pharmacy,
and the guy who repairs his carburetor.

He volunteers to repaint
the house she used to live in
a different color, sell it
to a stranger, some mean old crone,
or level it completely with a wrecking ball
the size of his disappointment.

Hoping to exact a purge through
rituals of elimination,
the gods might agree to expunge her
from his heart and mind,
taking him to that serene place
where forgetfulness cancels out hope.

Dear Jennifer Aniston

Heroic prototype of teary chick-flicks,
Ross's soulmate, and siren of the perfect hair,
today I confess to the tabloid's manufactured
success, stirring in me something
between crush and innocuous long-distance
stalking. I can't explain this desire to myself,
much less to friends or my spouse,
but I am compelled to purchase
every magazine in which your glossy image
appears on the cover, and while the photographs
inside tend always to look the same—Jennifer
on her stomach ankles crossed, Jennifer from deep
beneath her smooth waterfall of hair, Jennifer
pouting prettily as she contemplates
the scourge of cancer—I keep hoping to discover
explanations. I scour scrupulously
the stories behind your fame, praying
for epiphanies hidden underneath what Jennifer
eats, how Jennifer decorates her Hollywood
mansions, the importance of Jennifer's girl-
friends, will Jennifer ever get over Brad?
Same thing every time—I toss each magazine
in disappointment—until it finally dawned:
you've been my delicious forbidden fruit,
my sweet cream flavor
all along, American golden girl next door
whose husbands, brothers, and fathers
were so adamant we should never meet.

Tavern Portrait

You recognize trouble immediately
the moment she pours herself over to meet you,

open wine bottle in hand,
self-consciously proud of her accompanying

noise, bare midriff on display, half a ton of
eye makeup, wearing heels designed

for a younger woman, in spite of so many things
wrong, at the precipice of screaming

pay attention to me, damn it, and when you do
finally buy her a drink or six,

then you are introduced to the sadness
leaking out, cracking that crystalline party mask,

running down the sides of her once-pretty face,
like a fractured cubist painting. The dervish

spins uncontrollably because if it ever slowed
the entire façade would likely

collapse in on itself. And then,
you, and she, and maybe

everyone sitting in this dreary club might forget
it's Saturday night, deep into a deathless winter

and we all deserve at least some faith
in the possibility of resurrection.

Tonya Harding Agonistes

For Sherry Brown

Fierce warriors can overdose on adrenalin,
or too many second-place finishes,
directing boyfriend thug and leaden pipe
to lovely rival's knee.

Because she dared to do
what the rest of us only secretly project—

who among us dares to cast that first snowball?

Some sympathy, please,
for her subsequent free fall into obscurity,
the spotlight's frigid withdrawal:
female wrestling gigs in Berea, Ohio,
a "Greeter" at the local car wash—

tight wet tank top the job's only requirement.

Meanwhile, perfect alter ego,
America's virgin-n-cream unbottled brunette,
went spinning gold figure eights
on lucrative Disney on Ice contracts—

she who wore demure dresses and pearls

instead of pleather miniskirts,
sensible underwear instead of red thongs,
and did not once venture drunk
into the back seat of *any* boy's car.

In hindsight, some might argue,
Ms. Harding may have exercised consummate restraint
cracking only one of those sculpted legs.

Milton's fallen angels understood
the oppressive nature of Divine light
and no doubt shed sulfurous tears in Hell
that dark Olympic night
when Tonya's skate lace broke,
and with televised millions witnessed
such visible anguish in a woman's self-destruction,
her last chance skating away,

mascara-tinted tears, like ink blots on ice.

My McCarthy Era

I can no longer remember what she looked like,
how she smelled (although I recall
a decided preference for *L'Air du Temps*),

or why such an overwhelming hunger for her
compelled me to lift the telephone away from my ear
each time she began to talk about other boys.

That was my McCarthy era—not
so different, really, from that *other*
McCarthy era—figuring out how
to answer correctly and convincingly
barbed questions from my first serious girlfriend
who believed me capable of perpetual betrayal,
and whose cross-examinations would leave me
scared and breathless, wriggling as beneath
the business end of a pin.

She also let me kiss her places I'd only read about,

and that was the difference. My McCarthy
knew the power of sweetening hard inquiries
within the soft expanse of chestnut-colored hair
I was permitted to brush
in long, perfumed strokes,
sparking just enough red and gold highlights
until I was willing to confess
to everything she wanted to know.

Shadowland

She always knows more than anyone,
certainly more than me, about everything.
Thinks the world wouldn't dare kick her to the curb
just for growing old. Thinks she's
never going to die, not ever, that the spectacular beauty
she has grown accustomed to viewing
every morning in her vanity mirror
will hold as steadfastly immutable as her will.
She refuses to acknowledge all the little deaths
accumulating just outside her door.
What did she expect when she finally
opened that door and walked in on herself
suddenly 50? Did she think the magic coat
she inherited and that insulated her so well
would protect her forever, as if
time were as quaint as a cool spritz of spring rain,
some dry October leaves caught in the breeze?

Part Three: Innocent Abroad

Failure

With so many things to admire
it's easy to overlook the perseverance—
the getting up each morning to paint again,
to drink another cup of bitter coffee
and go back to work. This was long before
any of the work—yellow sun clusters
spackled to the blank faces of white canvas—
auctioned for millions of euros.

These days, he's off somewhere
shaking his head in befuddlement.
What he remembers is slightly less wonderful—
so much failure to overcome:
not lucky in love, not lucky with friends,
not lucky selling the damn paintings. Still,

he kept finding purple irises
rioting alongside the cracked wall of an asylum,
a haloed sower tossing sunflower seeds at barren soil,
the white explosions of peach blossoms
blooming hysterically in some absent farmer's orchard.

When the world finally recognized his achievement,
it had to divide it into pieces, painting
by painting, one or two per museum.
The other alternative, an entire room of rolling French
landscapes and flaming gardens in midsummer heat,
would likely blind the human eye
in a tsunami of color, ignite an internal
blaze, as it does daily in Amsterdam,
where the walls and ceilings must be asbestos-lined.

Visionaries find their own way;
legacies come from equal parts talent
and refusal to quit. While failure's specter
dogged him all the way into that wheatfield with crows,
he never forgot
in the time it took to stretch a canvas
and drop himself down into another painting,
for those hours at least,
beauty reigned.

Candyland

        I'm sitting
on a bench in the Rathhausplatz
in the middle of Augsburg, Germany,
in the middle of a delicious day in the middle of June
as weighted bells split the noon-hour air above me.

        Two young women
their tanned bodies barely contained
by white tank tops and the tiniest of shorts,
amuse one another with lithe blond laughter
as they mutually devour a bag of what must be
sickeningly-sweet red gobs of gelatinous candy.

        Trust me,
the last thing these two need
is more candy.

        Then, like frightened
pigeons alighting from cobblestones,
the sugar kicks in and they are up
and running in opposite directions—

one to jump the end car of a departing tram,
the other peddling her bicycle south.
They disappear like gossamer strands in a breeze.

        It's always
a little sad when you wake to the reality
you can no longer keep pace
with half the female population,
and that the other half now finds you invisible.

        Women think
they are the only ones
who grow invisible as they age.

But it's the way of a hard world,
and, in exchange, the gods sometimes provide
a few sweet bites of a blue-eyed Bavarian afternoon
for those left behind.

Why Language Matters

Sitting in a Munich *biergarten* next to four
young women who are smoking heavily and drinking

Coca-Cola and appear not to have
spoken to one another for years

instead of the hour that has elapsed
since their last cell phone communications,

I decide in a stunningly courageous overture
no doubt inspired by too much beer

and the halo of conviviality currently
engulfing the table, to introduce myself

in passable German that produces
a veritable blitzkrieg of questions

leading to my sheepish confession
I really don't speak much German

but do any of you speak English?
Nein. Polish and Russian are the other

fluencies tonight, and so I am consigned
to watch their conversation slip

back into the ease of its animated chatter
exiling me in a cloud of smoke.

Schattenboxen

The years drop a grey veil
over history, over the neat little
gold iron crosses that distinguish
war dead in Augsburg's cemetery,
where a blond boy's blood
stained the snow outside Moscow,
or splattered against this city's medieval wall.
Sixty years later, less the memory
of a generation, and visitors
must press harder still
to uncover evidence in these
sparkling streets and tipsy
beer gardens of what happened
right here.

He must have felt something
like psychic confirmation
residing atop the temple at Valhalla. Yet,
he never made it inside this hallowed place;
no marble bust for him resides
among the Teutonic gods Bismarck and Bach,
Goethe and Brahms, only one
for fierce little Sophie Scholl, who
resisted and was shot.
The world shrinks from the poster boy
of a retreating century awash
in his blood legacy, but no one
runs harder than his countrymen—
paranoid over the symbolism
of their flag, that some nationalist
refrain still lingers in the bars
of a soccer anthem. Who remains
more haunted by his ghost,
Deutschland or me? And when
does reparation signal repression, the

knowledge that his shadow
still lurks in a corner of the *hauptbahnof*,
a sneer pasted on that short upper
lip, awaiting a night train across the border
to some less ambivalent place.

From the Tongues of Strangers

It's graduation day at St. Stephans,
or it might be a wedding—my lame German makes either
a distinct possibility. A Bach concerto
rendered on an accordion serves as background music
for the many dressed-up high school students
gathering in the church courtyard below
each bearing attached parents, from whom the teenagers,
like all teenagers everywhere and always,
seek a quietly desperate escape.

The hard consonants of random conversations
sluice up to me in between Bach's notes.
I glean a few fragments—*mein sohn, ga neu,
sehr gut*—but my concentration fixes on the visuals:
men inserting index fingers into the perspiring gap
between necks and buttoned-up shirt collars,
women wearing gauzy summer dresses
negotiate the clipped and calculated movement
required for walking cobblestones in spike-heeled shoes.

Pedestrian passersby glance over into the courtyard,
smile, move on. As the true
stranger in this strange land,
I possess no such luxury. Everything I see here
pulls me in, as I slowly relearn the art of silence,
a particular offering available
to strangers alone abroad,
who must speak less than they understand
to appreciate that there are many languages
and only some of them use words.

On Viewing Brueghel's *Hunters in the Snow*

For Polly Binns

It hangs alone on its own wall,
Saal VIII, in the Kunsthistorisches, Vienna,
and although surrounded by other
equally famous Brueghels,
its stark aquas and whites
usurp command over the entire room.
Three hunters return from the woods
wearing a bowed fatigue that deepens in the
knowledge they have brought back the meat
of only a single red fox, enough barely
to feed the dogs. Perhaps Sunday afternoon
in February, an invisible sun
distributes its pale, even glow. The weary hunters
crest the last snow-covered ridge
on their way back into the village
where they have always lived
to find a familiar portrait: neighborhood children
playing winter games on frozen lakes,
one woman pulls another across the ice,
a stout Dutch matron on a bridge
carries bundled kindling home. The hunters' downcast eyes
notice neither the children nor the women,
and those below remain oblivious
to the hunters' return. In the distance
mountains powdered white with snow
snarl a mouthful of jagged teeth.

Collusion

While I was prowling the dank cathedral
basements and thousand-year-old cellars of Europe,
the woman charged with walking my American dog
sent an e-mail that my first-floor toilet

exploded last night, flooding our house
with a foot of water, an interior disaster
so epic it promises to rival Noah's.
I am writing this somewhere over the Atlantic,

the breadth of its ocean waters winking up at me
in all its aquamarine complacency,
while my restive dreamscape drifts out
to stroke the dark corners of my imagination,

taking me to visualized places
water has no business flowing, pooling over hardwood flooring,
cascading unabated down carpeted stairs. As if
water and my toilet shared a sinister collusion

to wait for a night when no one was home
and then, like fierce, unsupervised children,
unleashing a terrible surprise their sitter would find
the moment she stepped through the front door.

Reading Edgar

She introduced me to Mr. Poe
when I was just a boy, which is exactly
the right time to meet him, read to me
alone in the darkening quiet of the summer cottage
tales of desperate, sweating men
locked inside bedrooms and cellars
performing their full range of shameful pursuits
behind tightly drawn curtains.

        Her choice of Poe above others in the library
        baffles me still, and not the Poe
        of ratiocination, where the utterly linear
        Dupin deciphers every mystery
        with effortless superiority,
        as in the unfolding of a play.
        She chose instead the Poe of consuming consciousness,
        where ghosts honeycomb fevered brains.

She was the aunt who always
thought straight through to reason,
a cool voice of tranquil moderation
in a family of bubbling extremes. Perhaps she knew
without needing to explain
Poe was just another member of our
clan, a distant southern cousin,
issuing cautionary tales
none of us were ever smart enough to heed.

My Grandmother's Place

After my grandfather died,
my grandmother took
to spending most evenings

sitting in an overstuffed
leather chair in the corner
of a glassed-in sun porch.

While she read or knit,
the seasons passed inexorably around her,
as if she were a fixed body

and behind her, nature's changing
diurnal—rivulets of silver rain, the
fierce anarchy of blowing snow.

What has stayed with me on days
when I picture her alone in that room
is the slope of summer evenings

when the last kid has been called in
off the street and the sunlight
reaches down in a graceful arc

filtering its way through
errant openings among motionless leaves.
Did she ever look out

from behind her clean windows
and wonder the big questions
about where that sunlight

comes from, and where it goes,
about how much time
is left for any of us?

Or, was it enough just to know
her place in this room
gazing out into a well-kept yard

where the last of the light lingered
like white paint on darkening grass
for another minute more.

Frank Barone

Perhaps you remember your grandfather kindly?
Perhaps he even resembled old Kris Kringle
in appearance or attitude. Lucky you.
My grandfather, Frank Barone, gave me socks
for Christmas every year. Technically, he didn't
present the socks, his wife, my step-grandmother,
did. How could they have intuited
this was exactly what every twelve-year-old boy
wanted for Christmas: two sets of black argyle dress socks?
Frank Barone owned a '58 Ford Fairlane,
admittedly, not the sexiest car from that era
of sexy cars, but it had a cool push-button
gear selection system mounted on the dashboard.
When Frank Barone would get drunk
and my parents were out of sight,
he'd let me practice driving it up and down
the long driveway he hosed clean
after supper every summer night.
One day, Frank Barone got rear-ended in the Fairlane.
He wore a white Styrofoam neck-brace for two years
until the lawyers settled his case,
and then Frank Barone fixed the Fairlane and ditched
the white Styrofoam neck-brace.
As I was Frank Barone's only male heir,
he promised with witnesses present
the Fairlane would eventually go to me;
he'd have to die first, of course, but I held hope
of outliving him long enough to own it.
When a massive coronary surprised him one August,
I wore a pair of his Christmas socks
to St. Anthony's Church, and my mother
inquired his wife about the car.
She informed us the Fairlane was already gone,
sold to pay for Frank Barone's funeral.

Pool Table

Most of the time it sits there
Implacably alone, collecting dust in basement dark,
The heaviest thing in the house
Taking up too much space, holding up the big bag
Of dog food and clean laundry
Warm from inside the dryer's mouth.

Sometimes at night,
After we've had a few drinks and the mood
Is right, we stroke the length of its soft pelt
With a plush brush and turn it back
Into a glistening emerald pond.

The game changes depending on context
And participants: the bars and roadhouse
Pool, played beneath the rough hands
Of a working man's dirty fingers,

Abruptly becomes *Billiards* when paired
With a man leisurely smoking a cigar
And a woman in heels and upswept hair.

Either way, a unique assortment of gender cues—
Balls and holes, phallic sticks—as in croquet,
All meant to complement each other and coexist;
The orderly fulfillment of tenth-grade geometry
Where overly complicated mathematical proofs
Are redeemed in logical practicality
Assisted by the laws of physics—
A sphere set in motion collides with random objects in space
Propelling them into a black hole's planned extinction.

Head Down

> "In India, more people have cell phones
> than access to a toilet."
> *The New York Times Book Review*, May 27, 2012

On the bus last week
the heads of two dozen student riders
bowed in supplication to the virtual gods
Facebook and Twitter, enclosed in

identical yet singular acts of solipsistic reproduction,

while beyond mud-streaked bus windows
lurked nearly spring
replete with its halcyon subtleties:
white light splashing ubiquitously across the black elbows of trees

enclosed in identical yet singular acts of resurrection.

We must learn to temper our reverence
for technology, to locate its *off* switch,
an education that probably needs to occur
someplace other than inside the Verizon store,

where we might also train ourselves to view each new machine
like a toilet: conveyances possessing finite purposes—
to be employed when required,
followed by release from servitude.

Imagine your legitimate horror
if friend or spouse chose willfully to measure out
their remaining days within the confines of a diminutive
toilet stall, squandering precious hours

their head down, obliviously idled.

Then, the Letting Go

An afternoon nap that ambushed me
At the beach! I dreamed deeply of ocean,
Its massive aqua swells less impressive
Than the weight of its uniform silver.

An empty beach on a perfect
Summer day, except for my son and me
Walking beneath the transient shadows
Cast from high above as birds
And the occasional plastic bag
Somersaulted in the gentle breeze.

Nothing more than this,
I swear. Except that this time

When the usual sadness came to me
Over how much you would have
Appreciated joining us to walk
This long stretch of warm sand and sky,
There was no accompanying urge to look for you,

To interrupt what we were doing.
The sun on our faces, the sound of wind
Pursuing its implacable course into the future,
Leaving the past, like a glittering piece of glass
Discarded on the beach, meant to be examined,

But something to pass beyond,
Even if at the horizon
We could find no boats
And only the shadow of the day's encroaching end.

Part Four: Some Seasonal Excesses

Canada Snow Geese

1.48 a.m., a restive sleep
as we ride another year's autumnal wind
through the thousand maple leaves in
my front yard, like fingers through
so much old paper, and I think
was there ever a time
these serene blond birds and I
shared anything in common? Besides
of course the birthing and the dying
and the struggling in between.
In my mind I watch them
maintain their symmetrical V-formations
high above my house, pushing compulsively
south, their shrill staccato honking
an exotic fellowship
across an ocean of cold night air.

Early Season Frost

Early dark, mid December, snow falling
Alongside rapidly descending arc of dusk

When we stumble upon corner beauty salon open late,
Its lighted interior shining through glass windows

Made brighter still by two blond women
Their enormous hair piled up and out,

Like blooming stalks of yellow flowers, greenhouse cultivated,
Threaded with silver aluminum foil strips

As if prepped for electrification.
The imp in me cannot resist

Opening shop's plate glass door
(Warm puff of perfumed air billows out)

To apologize for our uninvited intrusion
But transformations are always worthy of notice.

The two beauticians and one blond customer
Laugh gloriously in apparent agreement or

Appreciation, but what is more interesting
Is the other seated woman who does not smile, choosing

Instead to send out wicked glare, as if winter's cold
Moved indoors instead of remaining out here with us.

Hurricane

What might have been just another
languid end-of-summer Sunday,
turns dire with meteorological prognostications
that propel anxious neighbors to grocery stores,
nervous retrievers to basement corners.

We follow bloated white mushroom on television radar
spinning counter-clockwise up the coast
bearing weighted bags of tropical bluster
that arrive like a busload of bad relatives,
flip the sodden leaves of maple trees inside out,
like women pulling themselves out of wet dresses.

At the bottom of my doomed street
some kid sits alone
inside the open mouth of his garage
pounding out a fierce syncopation
in an unrecognizable beat
on his metal drum set.

The Winterscapes of Stockholm's Prins Eugens Waldermarsudde Galleriet

We cling to whatever is most resilient to change.

Even the leaves in their annual march towards annihilation
Confirm a cycle. I want desperately to believe

Evidence of a God's design in winter's return,
Although as I write this, it's small, sharp teeth

Are elongating & straightening somewhere
In a dentist's office north of Manitoba.

No one knows what's out there better than the Swedes,
Whose snow paintings are absent of all delusion

Their singleness of season bearing down
With the relentlessness of a truck

Hauling heating oil or firewood.

You live in the Northlands long enough,
It's in the silver breath that slips out,

Like a confessional, between your own lips on a morning walk
Or, once the sun is down in October,

It's in the vapid air, chilled whiter than any wine,
Ready to purloin the last perfume of a fire burning

That lingers on tonight's early autumn breeze
So soft and unsuspecting, as in a first kiss,

Or the last.

Final Preparations

The last thing I must do:
the cleaning of the gutters
two stories high clinging
to the edge, a job
that waits patiently until
late November when the last
leaves are down, somehow
navigating their way into
such a narrow space. Only then
do I ascent the silver ladder
into the same color pewter sky
that whispers to me alone:
Better get a move on, boy,
you don't want to be up
this high when my winds
start blowing and the snow flies.

Gutters clogged with summer sludge,
the detritus of asphalt roofs,
and the maple leaves of autumn,
their colors like assorted candies,
rumpled brown dried crisp
and matted close, like some
hand has filed them tightly,
row-by-row, inside my gutter's
metal mouth that is forever open
as if awed by treetops and sky.

Afterwards,
there comes the ironic
spring-like washing of ice-cold hose
water running clear and unabated
along smooth silver bottoms,
so pure and clean you almost
expect to see fish—small orange

flames rushing headlong in celebration.

There is something wistful about
the cleaning of gutters:
another year's accumulation
and passing punctuated
by trips up and down the silver ladder,
each time, my feet a little less secure
atop the aging cylinder rungs
so high up above the ground
my sweatshirt stained with dirt
and the perspiration of fear,
my fingers red and numb
glad to be finished another year
with this task of winter, a measurement
to the nearness of endings.

Harbingers

Two poems unsettle my still-hibernating brain
this Sunday afternoon, shaking its sleepy quietude

          The first is a memory
of a girl before high school, Carol Richel,
whose father always had an eye looking
out their kitchen window watching me,

watching Carol walk
down the street on that first Spring day
warm enough for her to wear outside
black pantyhose and tight jean cut offs

short enough to impress us both
with how long Carol's legs had grown
over the length of the past winter.

          The second is a view
of my neighbor's yard from my kitchen window
as I watch him performing rituals to shake himself
from the frosty doldrums of March.

In his driveway he has constructed an altar
to future perfect tense: his red lawnmower,
a bag of black fertilizer, and a plastic hose

halfway unraveled from the green coil
that sleeps, like a snake, suffused in white light.

First Day of Winter

        Snow falling fast,
since daybreak, two feet equalizing everything
into the same lumpen mounds
of indiscernible white; trees and
bushes humbled by additional weight,
liberate their boughs in explosions
of misty powder.

        This is my third time
out today to add to the elevated
heaps on either side of my driveway
a roofless tunnel to the sky.

        The neighborhood kids
have had enough, retreated red-cheeked
and exhausted to Norman Rockwell kitchens, their
mothers' cups of steaming chocolate.

        It's just me
and winter left outside, alone in the driveway
the occasional beast of a yellow snowplow
rumbling along inside of blizzard of its own making,
leaving me another layer, heaviest of all,
just when I thought the work done.

        Watching weak afternoon die
inside a pewter sky empty of sun,
still white, except for my son's black leggings and hat
surmounting distant horizon,
snow-crusted golden retriever
trotting along at his side.

Day Spent Defining Superlatives

I. Try to imagine it this way: you spend
five months inside a closet; it's a spacious
closet—smells of cedar with great
shoes to look at and fondle—but it's nonetheless
still a closet. You take your meals in this closet,
shit in the closet, fuck in the closet, get dressed
and sleep in the closet until you are thoroughly
sick of the closet and the shoes inside,
regardless of how great they are. Then,
one day arrives this transfiguring light
the mind has until this moment lost
to blow apart the doors and walls of the closet
revealing the enormity of what lies beyond.

II. That first true afternoon of new Spring
when you sense the wolf has gone
back up north to sulk in its summer lair,
we put the top down and drove
up and down the concrete interstate.
The wind was cold in our hair and
against our faces, yet we knew another year's war
was finally finished. Overhead,
squawking snow geese casting shadowy
imprints along the length of frozen ground
told us the world had marked a change today.

III. The greatest gesture love has to offer
consists of more than earth and even flesh.
It is the gradual signaling of fresh spirit,
an unprepared transfusion
from the loins to the brain—
when the Spring overdue yesterday
arrives today. The greatest gesture of love
is anticipation, the absent touch
that revels in its longing,

the embodied reminders
that the sweetest part of any orange
is always the peeling.

Warm Summer Wind

To be sixteen or seventeen again, the world
still an exotic journey booked on a future itinerary
open to this glorious afternoon, late September,
in a lifetime of Septembers yet to come,
summer's fading light slipping through
rows of open windows and into
a long yellow school bus
as a high school girl's field hockey team
makes its way across the Interstate
to a game in some neighboring town.

My view inside the bus
lasts only a moment before we pass,
leaving its yellow bulk to shrink
within my rear-view mirror
as it recedes rapidly behind us.

But for that instant, I was one with the team
perched on an aisle seat
surrounded by much perfumed hair
pulled back into tight silken ponytails
in preparation for sport and sweat,
the last of the season's warm summer wind
twisting thin strands of brown and gold
that frame each lovely face,
more gentle than a hand's softest embrace.

Lesson Learned

His name was Benny and he had done serious time
in jail. The day he got out
he broke my nose on a soft October evening
my Senior year in high school
because I possessed the temerity
to ask out his hot girlfriend. In the back
of the Pizza Hut parking lot
in a corner between a stockade fence
and a black garbage dumpster,
giant pines looming up on either side,
I watched helplessly as his fury
escalated with each prefatory shove
until it bore down into lethal
frenzy—nostrils flaring,
breaths a staccato deepening,
even his stiff black hair was outraged
at this place where language had collapsed
and fists took over in a savage blur,
where midnight entered my sinuses
in the sharp tin taste of my own blood.
No longer able to see or breathe unencumbered,
I looked up at Benny and was afforded
a revelation, the inherent moral
attendant to dating any woman, regardless
how hot, who was the girlfriend
of a man who had escaped from a cage.

Vampire Redux

My vampire shops
at the same supermarket as me.
No surprise to find her there
late last night, my cart turning the corner
from the lurid red meat display
and into the sugar-flavored juice aisle.

>   Crimson lips and nails,
>   little black skirt, over-the-knee stiletto boots,
>   the same redundant retro fashion sense
>   plagiarized from Vampirella's Closet,

but still, looking finer than
any thousand-year-old revenant
had any right to be.

Stalking prey behind piled mounds of vegetables & fruits,
her smile, all sharpened canines,
no doubt expecting my acquiescence
& the usual delivery. You know

>   that look a vamp gets
>   when she's no longer listening to words,
>   hungry eyes zeroing in on a quivering

jugular. I should have staked her
right there on the cold linoleum floor,
but the juice aisle is located
on the other end of the store
from hardware.

We were interrupted by Father Rene,
grocery shopping for the orphanage kids,
or he might be the one
narrating this gothic interlude
as somber introduction
to a long-winded eulogy.

Watching Pornography

Talking is strictly optional;
why complicate events with context
when arousal is predicated
on a pair of silver-strapped stiletto heels,
a bubbly hot tub,
cue in some elevator music from Mexico,
and strangers are suddenly copulating everywhere
so flush and fleshy and friendly
it makes you self-conscious
to be in the same room
watching, the only person
who didn't get an invite to this party;
worse, the only one
still stuck inside clothes.

My Father's Cars

I. My father was not a cynical man.
But his critical balance
abandoned him every Friday afternoon
when his car was immersed in rush hour traffic
migrating north back to the suburbs, like angry salmon
trapped in spaces navigating an aggressive stream.

Sitting stiffly in the passenger seat
I would watch his anxiety level rise,
his hands strangling the wheel
each time another car
cut in front of his, or misused the break-
down lane out of selfish arrogance.
Look at these idiots, a pronouncement
meant for all four lanes of traffic.
Everybody in a big hurry to get home.
And for what? Drink a cold beer?
Fuck their wives? Even though I don't think
my father did much of either.

II. My father found artistic expression
in the automotive industry. For him,
cars were designed like flying buttress cathedrals:
both inside and out,
the bigger and more ostentatious,
the closer the owner came
to meeting the eye of God.

In the course of his lifetime,
he bought a series of Cadillacs and Oldsmobiles;
he never owned a car that wasn't forged
in Detroit. This wasn't so much evidence of patriotism,
as a desire for a motorized living room,
where he could rest his head on a cushioned seat
without my mother's complaining

he was getting head grease on her new upholstery.

III. My father was always generous with his toys.
I had access to his cars whenever I needed one—
he understood the importance of the backseat drama
playing at the local drive-in, appreciated as well
the sudden emanation of radiance
unfolding under a tight miniskirt
each time bare legs exploded from the front seat of his Cadillac.

What's Coming

I've seen the ending,
Not just that it will happen, as it must for each of us,
But *how*. I'll be attempting
To cross a slush-encumbered street in mid-winter.
It will be dusk, a purple evening.
This car, could be late-model white or red,
Will appear with its lights off
Driven by a teenage girl
With light brown hair, long and stringy,
In need of a shampoo, the strands surrounding her face
Always falling into her eyes, like Sissy Spacek
On the volleyball court in *Carrie*.
She will be preoccupied, snapping pink bubble gum,
Driving too fast down a short city block,
Reapplying strawberry-yum lip shine in the car's rear-view
Mirror, noting with dismay a localized acne outbreak,
Texting her boyfriend of two months,
Or perhaps her BFF, for a hook-up at a club,
And there I'll be inside destiny's cross-hairs,
Crossing the street at the wrong time
With my black school satchel
Filled with books, lunch bag, and poems.
Upon impact, we'll all go flying together,
Cartoon-like, up into the great beyond in one final
Awkward whelp. Maybe
The girl will stop to hover frantically,
Collect some poems—scattered like fresh snow
On the mounds of graying ice sludge
Piled up on either side of the street.
She won't end up reading them, however,
Unable to concentrate beyond
The major inconvenience
This moment is going to turn out to be.

Entanglements

Moist little fists at the tip ends of bare black branches open
each perfect and glistening like small verdant trumpets,
relatives summon you back home
to begin the vigil of your father's hospice stay.

The need to explore her mouth again
distracts mightily from the ability to concentrate elsewhere,
the novel concludes in an unexpected resolution;
it will require time to digest.

A full moon rides the ethereal edges of white clouds,
light so bright through your window, it summons you awake,
the tornado cuts a devastating swath through the town's center,
the first building the townspeople rebuild is their church.

It is your first time behind the wheel,
accelerating up the expressway ramp, the horizon beckons,
the old dog with cataracts sluicing both eyes
descends tentatively down each basement stair.

Two teenagers, beautiful in their adult awkwardness,
exit the hotel on the way to their Senior prom,
when you tell them *it won't get much better than this*,
only the girl nods back her silent understanding.

The smell of fresh cut grass in May is thick and redolent,
its blades bleed your sneakers and bare ankles green,
the leaves on the corner oak tree are the last to go
their uniform brown rustles like old paper in the wind.

Your high school girlfriend sends you a picture
of her lovely daughter on her twenty-fifth birthday,
the photograph takes you back to a photograph of her mother
forty years ago, younger than her daughter is today.

Sure signs of ageing: a fresh sensitivity to endings,
the daily additions to the list of things you are going to miss.
Take a long trip to a mysterious place.
Scare yourself so hard it translates into gratitude.

Acknowledgements

Some of these poems were originally published elsewhere and in somewhat different forms. The author gratefully acknowledges here the editors and journals where they first appeared:

"Failure" *Literary Laundry*

"Vampire Redux" *Seven Days*

"San Diego" *Northern New England Review*

"First Day of Winter" *Blueline*

"Final Preparations" *Blueline*

"Crime Scene" *Cultural Weekly*

Fomite
Burlington, Vermont

Fomite is a literary press whose authors and artists explore the human condition—political, cultural, personal and historical—in poetry and prose.

A fomite is a medium capable of transmitting infectious organisms from one individual to another.

"The activity of art is based on the capacity of people to be infected by the feelings of others." Tolstoy, *What is Art?*

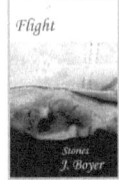

Flight and Other Stories - Jay Boyer
In *Flight and Other Stories,* we're with the fattest woman on earth as she draws her last breaths and her soul ascends toward its final reward. We meet a divorcee who can fly for no more effort than flapping her arms. We follow a middle-aged butler whose love affair with a young woman leads him first to the mysteries of bondage, and then to the pleasures of malice. Story by story, we set foot into worlds so strange as to seem all but surreal, yet everything feels familiar, each moment rings true. And that's when we recognize we're in the hands of one of America's truly original talents.

Loisaida - Dan Chodorokoff
Catherine, a young anarchist estranged from her parents and squatting in an abandoned building on New York's Lower East Side is fighting with her boyfriend and conflicted about her work on an underground newspaper. After learning of a developer's plans to demolish a community garden, Catherine builds an alliance with a group of Puerto Rican community activists. Together they confront the confluence of politics, money, and real estate that rule Manhattan. All the while she learns important lessons from her great-grandmother's life in the Yiddish anarchist movement that flourished on the Lower East Side at the turn of the century. In this coming of age story, family saga, and tale of urban politics, Dan Chodorkoff explores the "principle of hope", and examines how memory and imagination inform social change.

Improvisational Arguments - Anna Faktorovich
Improvisational Arguments is written in free verse to capture the essence of modern problems and triumphs. The poems clearly relate short, frequently humorous and occasionally tragic, stories about travels to exotic and unusual places, fantastic realms, abnormal jobs, artistic innovations, political objections, and misadventures with love.

Loosestrife - Greg Delanty
This book is a chronicle of complicity in our modern lives, a witnessing of war and the destruction of our planet. It is also an attempt to adjust the more destructive blueprint myths of our society. Often our cultural memory tells us to keep quiet about the aspects that are most challenging to our ethics, to forget the violations we feel and tremors that keep us distant and numb.

Fomite
Burlington, Vermont

Carts and Other Stories - Zdravka Evtimova

Roots and wings are the key words that best describe the short story collection, Carts and Other Stories, by Zdravka Evtimova. The book is emotionally multilayered and memorable because of its internal power, vitality and ability to touch both the heart and your mind. Within its pages, the reader discovers new perspectives and true wealth, and learns to see the world with different eyes. The collection lives on the borders of different cultures. Carts and Other Stories will take the reader to wild and powerful Bulgarian mountains, to silver rains in Brussels, to German quiet winter streets and to wind bitten crags in Afghanistan. This book lives for those seeking to discover the beauty of the world around them, and will have them appreciating what they have—and perhaps what they have lost as well.

The Listener Aspires to the Condition of Music - Barry Goldensohn

"I know of no other selected poems that selects on one theme, but this one does, charting Goldensohn's career-long attraction to music's performance, consolations and its august, thrilling, scary and clownish charms. Does all art aspire to the condition of music as Pater claimed, exhaling in a swoon toward that one class act? Goldensohn is more aware than the late 19th century of the overtones of such breathing: his poems thoroughly round out those overtones in a poet's lifetime of listening."
John Peck, poet, editor, Fellow of the American Academy of Rome

The Co-Conspirator's Tale - Ron Jacobs

There's a place where love and mistrust are never at peace; where duplicity and deceit are the universal currency. The Co-Conspirator's Tale takes place within this nebulous firmament. There are crimes committed by the police in the name of the law. Excess in the name of revolution. The combination leaves death in its wake and the survivors struggling to find justice in a San Francisco Bay Area noir by the author of the underground classic The Way the Wind Blew: A History of the Weather Underground and the novel Short Order Frame Up.

Short Order Frame Up - Ron Jacobs

1975. America has lost its war in Vietnam and Cambodia. Racially-tinged riots are tearing the city of Boston apart. The politics and counterculture of the 1960s is disintegrating into nothing more than sex, drugs and rock and roll. The Boston Red Sox are on one of their improbable runs toward a postseason appearance. In a suburban town in Maryland, a young couple is murdered and another young man is accused. The couple are white and the accused is black. It is up to his friends and family to prove he is innocent. This is a story of suburban ennui, race, murder and injustice. Religion and politics, liberal lawyers and racist cops. In Short Order Frame Up, Ron Jacobs has written a piece of crime fiction that exposes the wound that is US racism. Two cultures existing side by side and across generations--a river very few dare to cross. His characters work and live with and next to each other, often unaware of the other's real life. When the murder occurs, however, those people that care about the man charged must cross that river and meet somewhere in between in order to free him from (what is to them) an obvious miscarriage of justice.

Fomite
Burlington, Vermont

All the Sinners Saints - Ron Jacobs
A young draftee named Victor Willard goes AWOL in Germany after an altercation with a commanding officer. Porgy is an African-American GI involved with the international Black Panthers and German radicals. Victor and a female radical named Ana fall in love. They move into Ana's room in a squatted building near the US base in Frankfurt. The international campaign to free Black revolutionary Angela Davis is coming to Frankfurt. Porgy and Ana are key organizers and Victor spends his days and nights selling and smoking hashish, while becoming addicted to heroin. Police and narcotics agents are keeping tabs on them all. Politics, love, and drugs. Truths, lies, and rock and roll. *All the Sinners, Saints* is a story of people seeking redemption in a world awash in sin.

When You Remember Deir Yassin - R.L. Green
When You Remember Deir Yassin is a collection of poems by R. L. Green, an American Jewish writer, on the subject of the occupation and destruction of Palestine. Green comments: "Outspoken Jewish critics of Israeli crimes against humanity have, strangely, been called 'anti-Semitic' as well as the hilariously illogical epithet 'self-hating Jews.' As a Jewish critic of the Israeli government, I have come to accept these accusations as a stamp of approval and a badge of honor, signifying my own fealty to a central element of Jewish identity and ethics: one must be a lover of truth and a friend to the oppressed, and stand with the victims of tyranny, not with the tyrants, despite tribal loyalty or self-advancement. These poems were written as expressions of outrage, and of grief, and to encourage my sisters and brothers of every cultural or national grouping to speak out against injustice, to try to save Palestine, and in so doing, to reclaim for myself my own place as part of the Jewish people." Poems in the original English are accompanied by Arabic and Hebrew translations.

Roadworthy Creature, Roadworthy Craft - Kate Magill
Words fail but the voice struggles on. The culmination of a decade's worth of performance poetry, *Roadworthy Creature, Roadworthy Craft* is Kate Magill's first full-length publication. In lines that are sinewy yet delicate, Magill's poems explore the terrain where idea and action meet, where bodies and words commingle to form a strange new flesh, a breathing text, an "I" that spirals outward from itself.

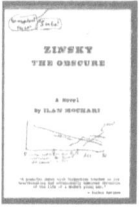

Zinsky the Obscure - Ilan Mochari
"If your childhood is brutal, your adulthood becomes a daily attempt to recover: a quest for ecstasy and stability in recompense for their early absence." So states the 30-year-old Ariel Zinsky, whose bachelor-like lifestyle belies the torturous youth he is still coming to grips with. As a boy, he struggles with the beatings themselves; as a grownup, he struggles with the world's indifference to them. *Zinsky the Obscure* is his life story, a humorous chronicle of his search for a redemptive ecstasy through sex, an entrepreneurial sports obsession, and finally, the cathartic exercise of writing it all down. Fervently recounting both the comic delights and the frightening horrors of a life in which he feels—always—that he is not like all the rest, Zinsky survives the worst and relishes the best with idiosyncratic style, as his heartbreak turns into self-awareness and his suicidal ideation into self-regard. A vivid evocation of the all-consuming nature of lust and ambition—and the forces that drive them.

Fomite
Burlington, Vermont

The Derivation of Cowboys & Indians - Joseph D. Reich

The Derivation of Cowboys & Indians represents a profound journey, a breakdown of The American Dream from a social, cultural, historical, and spiritual point of view. Reich examines in concise detail the loss of the collective unconscious, commenting on our contemporary postmodern culture with its self-interested excesses, on where and how things all go wrong, and how social/political practice rarely meets its original proclamations and promises. Reich's surreal and self-effacing satire brings this troubling message home. *The Derivations of Cowboys & Indians* is a desperate search and struggle for America's literal, symbolic, and spiritual home.

Kasper Planet: Comix and Tragix - Peter Schumann

The British call him Punch, the Italians, Pulchinella, the Russians, Petruchka, the Native Americans, Coyote. These are the figures we may know. But every culture that worships authority will breed a Punch-like, anti-authoritarian resister. Yin and yang—it has to happen. The Germans call him Kasper. Truth-telling and serious pranking are dangerous professions when going up against power. Bradley Manning sits naked in solitary; Julian Assange is pursued by Interpol, Obama's Department of Justice, and Amazon.com. But —in contrast to merely human faces— masks and theater can often slip through the bars. Consider our American Kaspers: Charlie Chaplin, Woody Guthrie, Abby Hoffman, the Yes Men—theater people all, utilizing various forms to seed critique. Their profiles and tactics have evolved along with those of their enemies. Who are the bad guys that call forth the Kaspers? Over the last half century, with his Bread & Puppet Theater, Peter Schumann has been tireless in naming them, excoriating them with Kasperdom....
from Marc Estrin's Foreword to Planet Kasper

Views Cost Extra - L.E. Smith

Views that inspire, that calm, or that terrify—all come at some cost to the viewer. In *Views Cost Extra* you will find a New Jersey high school preppy who wants to inhabit the "perfect" cowboy movie, a rural mailman disgusted with the residents of his town who wants to live with the penguins, an ailing screen writer who strikes a deal with Johnny Cash to reverse an old man's failures, an old man who ponders a young man's suicide attempt, a one-armed blind blues singer who wants to reunite with the car that took her arm on the assembly line— and more. These stories suggest that we must pay something to live even ordinary lives.

The Empty Notebook Interrogates Itself - Susan Thomas

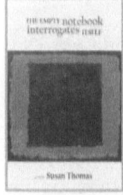

The Empty Notebook began its life as a very literal metaphor for a few weeks of what the poet thought was writer's block, but was really the struggle of an eccentric persona to take over her working life. It won. And for the next three years everything she wrote came to her in the voice of the Empty Notebook, who, as the notebook began to fill itself, became rather opinionated, changed gender, alternately acted as bully and victim, had many bizarre adventures in exotic locales and developed a somewhat politically-incorrect attitude. It then began to steal the voices and forms of other poets and tried to immortalize itself in various poetry reviews. It is now thrilled to collect itself in one slim volume.

Fomite
Burlington, Vermont

My God, What Have We Done? - Susan Weiss

In a world afflicted with war, toxicity, and hunger, does what we do in our private lives really matter? Fifty years after the creation of the atomic bomb at Los Alamos, newlyweds Pauline and Clifford visit that once-secret city on their honeymoon, compelled by Pauline's fascination with Oppenheimer, the soulful scientist. The two stories emerging from this visit reverberate back and forth between the loneliness of a new mother at home in Boston and the isolation of an entire community dedicated to the development of the bomb. While Pauline struggles with unforeseen challenges of family life, Oppenheimer and his crew reckon with forces beyond all imagining.

Finally the years of frantic research on the bomb culminate in a stunning test explosion that echoes a rupture in the couple's marriage. Against the backdrop of a civilization that's out of control, Pauline begins to understand the complex, potentially explosive physics of personal relationships.

At once funny and dead serious, *My God, What Have We Done?* sifts through the ruins left by the bomb in search of a more worthy human achievement.

As It Is On Earth - Peter M. Wheelwright

Four centuries after the Reformation Pilgrims sailed up the down-flowing watersheds of New England, Taylor Thatcher, irreverent scion of a fallen family of Maine Puritans, is still caught in the turbulence.

In his errant attempts to escape from history, the young college professor is further unsettled by his growing attraction to Israeli student Miryam Bluehm as he is swept by Time through the "family thing"—from the tangled genetic and religious history of his New England parents to the redemptive birthday secret of Esther Fleur Noire Bishop, the Cajun-Passamaquoddy woman who raised him and his younger half-cousin/half-brother, Bingham.

The landscapes, rivers, and tidal estuaries of Old New England and the Mayan Yucatan are also casualties of history in Thatcher's story of Deep Time and re-discovery of family on Columbus Day at a high-stakes gambling casino, rising in resurrection over the starlit bones of a once-vanquished Pequot Indian Tribe.

Suite for Three Voices - Derek Furr

Suite for Three Voices is a dance of prose genres, teeming with intense human life in all its humor and sorrow. A son uncovers the horrors of his father's wartime experience, a hitchhiker in a muumuu guards a mysterious parcel, a young man foresees his brother's brush with death on September 11. A Victorian poetess encounters space aliens and digital archives, a runner hears the voice of a dead friend in the song of an indigo bunting, a teacher seeks wisdom from his students' errors and Neil Young. By frozen waterfalls and neglected graveyards, along highways at noon and rivers at dusk, in the sound of bluegrass, Beethoven, and Emily Dickinson, the essays and fiction in this collection offer moments of vision.

Fomite
Burlington, Vermont

Travers' Inferno - L.E. Smith

In the 1970's churches began to burn in Burlington, Vermont. If it were arson, no one or no reason could be found to blame. This book suggests arson, but makes no claim to historical realism. It claims, instead, to capture the dizzying 70's zeitgeist of aggressive utopian movements, distrust in authority, escapist alternative life styles, and a bewildered society of onlookers. In the tradition of John Gardner's Sunlight Dialogues, the characters of *Travers' Inferno* are colorful and damaged, sometimes comical, sometimes tragic, looking for meaning through desperate acts. Travers Jones, the protagonist, is grounded in the transcendent—philosophy, epilepsy, arson as purification—and mystified by the opposite sex, haunted by an absent father and directed by an uncle with a grudge. He is seduced by a professor's wife and chased by an endearing if ineffective sergeant of police. There are secessionist Quebecois involved in these church burns who are murdering as well as pilfering and burning. There are changing alliances, violent deaths, lovemaking, and a belligerent cat.

Still Time - Michael Cocchiarale

Still Time is a collection of twenty-five short and shorter stories exploring tensions that arise in a variety of contemporary relationships: a young boy must deal with the wrath of his out-of-work father; a woman runs into a man twenty years after an awkward sexual encounter; a wife, unable to conceive, imagines her own murder, as well as the reaction of her emotionally distant husband; a soon-to-be tenured English professor tries to come to terms with her husband's shocking return to the religion of his youth; an assembly line worker, married for thirty years, discovers the surprising secret life of his recently hospitalized wife. Whether a few hundred or a few thousand words, these and other stories in the collection depict characters at moments of deep crisis. Some feel powerless, overwhelmed—unable to do much to change the course of their lives. Others rise to the occasion and, for better or for worse, say or do the thing that might transform them for good. Even in stories with the most troubling of endings, there remains the possibility of redemption. For each of the characters, there is still time.

Signed Confessions - Tom Walker

Guilt and a desperate need to repent drive the antiheroes in Tom Walker's dark (and often darkly funny) stories:
- A gullible journalist falls for the 40-year-old stripper he profiles in a magazine.
- A faithless husband abandons his family and joins a support group for lost souls.
- A merciless prosecuting attorney grapples with the suicide of his gay son.
- An aging misanthrope must make amends to five former victims.
- An egoistic naval hero is haunted by apparitions of his dead wife and a mysterious little girl.

The seven tales in *Signed Confessions* measure how far guilty men will go to obtain a forgiveness no one can grant but themselves.

Fomite
Burlington, Vermont

The Good Muslim of Jackson Heights - Jaysinh Birjépatil
Jackson Heights in this book is a fictional locale with common features assembled from immigrant-friendly neighborhoods around the world where hardworking honest-to-goodness traders from the Indian subcontinent, rub shoulders with ruthless entrepreneurs, reclusive antique-dealers, homeless nobodies, merchant-princes, lawyers, doctors and IT specialists. But as Siraj and Shabnam, urbane newcomers fleeing religious persecution in their homeland discover there is no escape from the past. Weaving together the personal and the political *The Good Muslim of Jackson Heights* is an ambiguous elegy to a utopian ideal set free from all prejudice.

Meanwell - Janice Miller Potter
Meanwell is a twenty-four poem sequence in which a female servant searches for identity and meaning in the shadow of her mistress, poet Anne Bradstreet. Although Meanwell herself is a fiction, someone like her could easily have existed among Bradstreet's known but unnamed domestic servants. Through Meanwell's eyes, Bradstreet emerges as a human figure during The Great Migration of the 1600s, a period in which the Massachusetts Bay Colony was fraught with physical and political dangers. Through Meanwell, the feelings of women, silenced during the midwife Anne Hutchinson's fiery trial before the Puritan ministers, are finally acknowledged. In effect, the poems are about the making of an American rebel. Through her conflicted conscience, we witness Meanwell's transformation from a powerless English waif to a mythic American who ultimately chooses wilderness over the civilization she has experienced.

The Housing Market - Joseph D. Reich
In Joseph Reich's most recent social and cultural, contemporary satire of suburbia entitled, "The Housing market: a comfortable place to jump off the end of the world," the author addresses the absurd, postmodern elements of what it means, or for that matter not, to try and cope and function, and survive and thrive, or live and die in the repetitive and existential, futile and self-destructive, homogenized, monochromatic landscape of a brutal and bland, collective unconscious, which can spiritually result in a gradual wasting away and erosion of the senses or conflict and crisis of a desperate, disproportionate 'situational depression,' triggering and leading the narrator to feel constantly abandoned and stranded, more concretely or proverbially spoken, "the eternal stranger," where when caught between the fight or flight psychological phenomena, naturally repels him and causes him to flee and return without him even knowing it into the wild, while by sudden circumstance and coincidence discovers it surrounds the illusory-like circumference of these selfsame Monopoly board cul-de-sacs and dead ends. Most specifically, what can happen to a solitary, thoughtful, and independent thinker when being stagnated in the triangulation of a cookie-cutter, oppressive culture of a homeowner's association; A memoir all written in critical and didactic, poetic stanzas and passages, and out of desperation, when freedom and control get taken, what he is forced to do in the illusion of 'free will and volition,' something like the derivative art of a smart and ironic and social and cultural satire.

Fomite
Burlington, Vermont

Love's Labours - Jack Pulaski
In the four stories and two novellas that comprise Love's Labors the protagonists Ben and Laura, discover in their fervid romance and long marriage their interlocking fates, and the histories that preceded their births. They also learned something of the paradox between love and all the things it brings to its beneficiaries: bliss, disaster, duty, tragedy, comedy, the grotesque, and tenderness.

Ben and Laura's story is also the particularly American tale of immigration to a new world. Laura's story begins in Puerto Rico, and Ben's lineage is Russian-Jewish. They meet in City College of New York, a place at least analogous to a melting pot. Laura struggles to rescue her brother from gang life and heroin. She is mother to her younger sister; their mother Consuelo is the financial mainstay of the family and consumed by work. Despite filial obligations, Laura aspires to be a serious painter. Ben writes, cares for and is caught up in the misadventures and surreal stories of his younger schizophrenic brother. Laura is also a story teller as powerful and enchanting as Scheherazade. Ben struggles to survive such riches, and he and Laura endure.

Four-Way Stop - Sherry Olson
If *Thank You* were the only prayer, as Meister Eckhart has suggested, it would be enough, and Sherry Olson's poetry, in her second book, *Four-Way Stop*, would be one. Radical attention, deep love, and dedication to kindness illuminate these poems and the stories she tells us, which are drawn from her own life: with family, with friends, and wherever she travels, with strangers – who to Olson, never are strangers, but kin.

Even at the difficult intersections, as in the title poem, *Four-Way Stop*, Olson experiences – and offers – hope, showing us how, *completely unsupervised*, people take turns, with *kindness waving each other on*. Olson writes, knowing that (to quote Czeslaw Milosz)) *What surrounds us, here and now, is not guaranteed*. To this world, with her poems, Olson brings – and teaches – attention, generosity, compassion, and appreciative joy.
—Carol Henrikson

Raven or Crow - Joshua Amses
Marlowe has recently moved back home to Vermont after flunking his first term at a private college in the Midwest, when his sort of girlfriend, Eleanor, goes missing. The circumstances surrounding Eleanor's disappearance stand to reveal more about Marlowe than he is willing to allow. Rather than report her missing, he resolves to find Eleanor himself. *Raven or Crow* is the story of mistakes rooted in the ambivalence of being young and without direction.

Alfabestiario
AlphaBetaBestiario - Antonello Borra
Animals have always understood that mankind is not fully at home in the world. Bestiaries, hoping to teach, send out warnings. This one, of course, aims at doing the same.

Fomite
Burlington, Vermont

Visiting Hours - *Jennifer Anne Moses*
Visiting Hours, a novel-in-stories, explores the lives of people not normally met on the page—-AIDS patients and those who care for them. Set in Baton Rouge, Louisiana, and written with large and frequent dollops of humor, the book is a profound meditation on faith and love in the face of illness and poverty.

Did you know that you can write a review on Amazon, Good Reads or Shelfari? Just go to the book page on the website and follow the links for posting a review. Books from independent presses depend on reader to reader communications.

www.ingramcontent.com/pod-product-compliance
Lightning Source LLC
Chambersburg PA
CBHW030331080526
44584CB00012B/809